Sight Reading Complete for Drummers

for Drummers

Volume 3 of 3

By Mike Prestwood

An exploration of rhythm, notation, technique, and musicianship

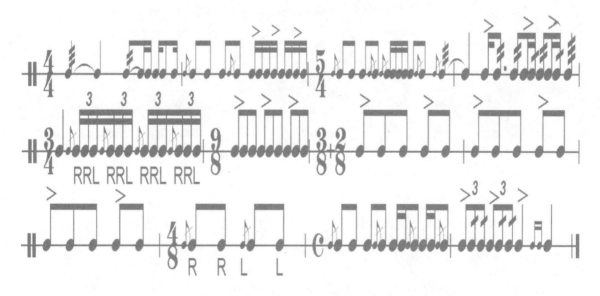

ISBN 0-9760928-2-4

Published By
Prestwood Publications
www.prestwoodpublications.com

Exclusively Distributed By
Play-Drums.com
www.play-drums.com

Sight Reading Complete for Drummers © 1984, 2004 Mike Prestwood. All Rights Reserved

Dedication

I dedicate this method series to my first drum instructor Joe Santoro. Joe is a brilliant instructor and an exceptional percussionist. With his guidance, I progressed quickly and built a foundation for a lifetime of drumming fueled by his encouragement and enthusiasm.

Copy Editor : Leslie Prestwood
Cover Design: Patrick Ramos
Cover Photography: Michelle Walker
Music Engraving: Mike Prestwood
Special thanks to James LaRheir

Contents

Introduction 1

Lesson 1: Common Rhythm Review / Sticking Styles 2

Lesson 2: Duplets (2's) and Quadruplets (4's).......................3

Lesson 3: Quintuplets (5's) and Septuplets (7's)..................5

Lesson 4: Refining Triple Strokes 7

Lesson 5: 32nd Note Singles 9

Lesson 6: Alternative Notation 11

Lesson 7: Advanced Time Signatures 14

Lesson 8: 64th Notes in 16th Note Time Signatures............20

Lesson 9: 128th Notes in 32nd Note Time Signatures 21

Lesson 10: Odd Time Rhythmic Review................................22

Lesson 11: Prime Numbers and Rhythm 23

Lesson 12: Rhythmic Mnemonics 24

Lesson 13: Easy Breakdowns 25

Lesson 14: Advanced ¼ Note Triplet Exercises 28

Lesson 15: Advanced Tuples..29

Lesson 16: Tuple Problem Areas 41

Lesson 17: Shifting Beat Groups 44

Lesson 18: Switching Beat Duration (Same Beat Count)...45

Lesson 19: Switching Beat Duration.....................................46

Lesson 20: No Time Signature..50

Lesson 21: Flat Flams and Polyrhythms 51

Appendix A: Warm-Up Set 3 53

Appendix B: Mixed Rhythm Accent Patterns.......................56

Appendix C: Final Snare Solo..59

Introduction

Volume 3 is the final volume of this 3-volume series and it explores advanced rhythm and notation concepts. The snare solo titled, "Kitchen Sink" at the end of this book reviews nearly all the material from all three volumes of this series. It groups elements into sections. Kitchen Sink is an excellent review piece and, for teachers, it is an excellent placement test.

Getting the Most Out of this Book

As in volume 2, most of the exercises in this volume specify both practice tempo and dynamics, either in the music (using traditional notation marks) or in the lesson description. Practice the tempos and dynamics specified, then other tempos as desired. To get the most out of each exercise, play the exercises several times alternating between playing the exercises with a metronome, with no metronome, and with the audio files.

The first time through, proceed straight through all 21 lessons in volume three. Start each practice session with a warm up using Appendix A of this volume, and build your chops using Appendix B as written or using one of the variations.

Review: After completing the lessons in this method series, you can use these books for review material and chop building. If you own all three volumes of this series, here is a formula for getting the most out of them:

1. **Warm Up** - Warm up using Appendix A of any one volume. The volume 1 warm up is quick and easy while the warm ups in volumes 2 and 3 (this volume) are more complex. Strive for loose and relaxed muscles.

2. **Build Your Chops** – Build your chops using Appendix B of any one volume.

3. **Take a Lesson** - Choose one lesson from each volume (three lessons total) and review the material thoroughly. Strive for a very high quality musical sound.

Legend

The following is a legend for this three volume series:

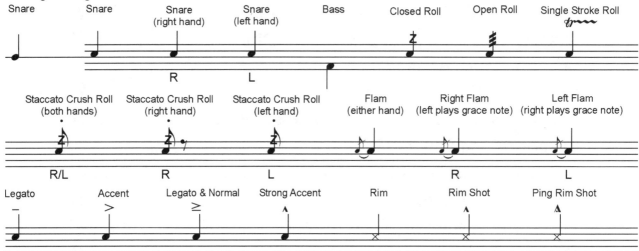

Play-Drums.com

You will find supplemental information at the following internet address:

www.play-drums.com/sightreading

This is the official website for this series and includes free movies that demonstrate various techniques included in this series as well as related material such as marching snare, drum set playing, and other exercises.

Download the MP3 Audio Files

In order to perfect your timing and ability to play at various tempos, you need to hear the rhythms and play along with them. Free MP3 audio files for the lessons in this series are available for download. You can play them on your computer, download them to your MP3 player, or burn them to CD. Get the files now at

www.play-drums.com/sightreading/download

Here is a guide to the file naming convention:

- **3-Lesson + ## + Ex + ## + ### BPM** = The exercise(s) at the given tempo. This will either be snare only or snare and bass depending on the exercise.

- **Bass** = If "Bass" is indicated, then this version is the bass drum only part which is helpful with learning to play along with other instruments.

- **Click** = If "Click" is indicated, then this version is a click track at the given tempo. These versions are particularly helpful with the time switching exercises.

- **Check** = If "Check" is indicated, this version contains a rhythmic check pattern. This is particularly helpful with the timing and accent exercises.

Online Message Board

Post your questions and comments on our message board.

Online Teacher Guide

An online teacher's guide is available at play-drums.com.

Lesson 1: Common Rhythm Review / Sticking Styles

This lesson serves the dual purpose of common rhythm review and a review of two common sticking styles: right hand lead and alternating. With the right hand lead style, you use your right hand for downbeats and the left hand for upbeats. You might find right hand lead is easier to play because you play the same rhythms using the same sticking each time. I suggest you master both styles of sticking. Which you use in performance is up to you so long as you play with confidence. Play each exercise at the three tempos specified and using both sticking patterns.

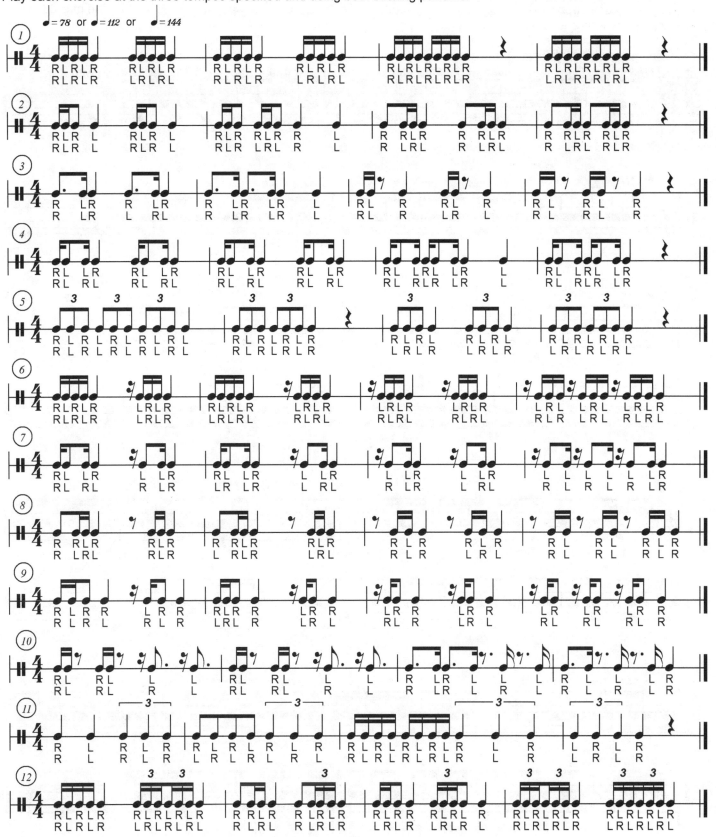

Lesson 2: Duplets (2's) and Quadruplets (4's)

Duplets, like triplets, are a type of tuple (an irregular note division). Typically, you play a duplet (two notes) in the place of three notes. For example, in compound 8th note time signatures like $\frac{6}{8}$, you play an eighth note duplet in the space of three eighths. A *quadruplet* is a grouping of four notes. In $\frac{6}{8}$, you can play a 16th note quadruplet (four notes) in the space of six 16th notes. The first two exercises use the clearer ratio notation. Exercise #4 uses dotted 8ths and 16ths to notate duplets and quadruplets. The use of dotted 8ths and 16ths is rhythmically correct and is common with many composers. The rest of the exercises use the traditional notation for tuples. You can read the ratio notation for exercise #1 as play two notes in the place of three 8th notes, and you can read exercise #2 as play four notes in the place of six 16th notes.

Lesson 3: Quintuplets (5's) and Septuplets (7's)

Quintuplets and *septuplets*, like triplets and duplets, are irregular note divisions (types of tuples). You play a quintuplet (5 notes) and a septuplet (7 notes) in the same duration as another note or set of notes. For example, in $\frac{4}{4}$ you can play a 16th note quintuplet (5 notes) in the place of one quarter note. Although you can use mnemonics with slow tempos to get the feel of 5's and 7's, most drummers do not count 5's and 7's because you usually play them too fast to count.

Quintuplets

Septuplets

When you play a single triplet, quintuplet, or septuplet, you switch from hand to hand. Exercise #1 and #3 stress the use of two of the same tuples in a row and exercises #2 and #4 mix it up. Keep in mind which hand you are starting on and ending on. Exercises #2 and #3 use the clearer ratio notation while the rest of the exercises use the traditional notation. You can read the ratio notation used in exercises #2 and #3 as play five notes in the place of four 16th notes, play three notes in the place of two 8th notes, and play seven notes in the place four 16th notes.

This next exercise is a very difficult exercise. It stresses replacing either two or three notes with either a quintuplet or a septuplet. To be clear, the quintuplet in measure 7 replaces three eighth notes and the quintuplet in measure 19 replaces two eighth notes (and is a bit faster). To perfect your timing, download the MP3 files from play-drums.com and play along with them.

Lesson 4: Refining Triple Strokes

This lesson builds on the lesson titled "Triple Strokes" in Volume 2. The purpose of this lesson is to develop fast and controlled triple strokes. Exercises 5 and 6 are a bit insane but fun to practice at slow speeds and will build your confidence playing triple strokes at a more reasonable tempo and rhythm pattern. Exercise #2 uses the older slur bracket style you may occasionally come across. Exercise 6 uses the newer square bracket. Composers use brackets, whether slurs or square, to clarify which notes belong to the tuple (in this case triplets and 9-tuples).

Practice variation You can practice this lesson using only single strokes, too.

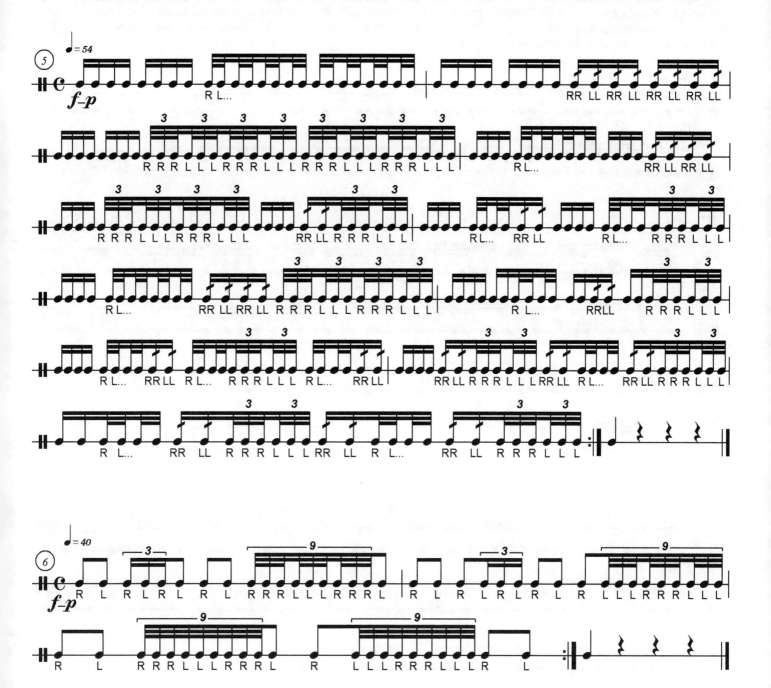

Lesson 5: 32nd Note Singles

With this lesson, you develop fast 32nd note singles in common time and $\frac{3}{4}$ time. For a more rudimental approach, you can use double strokes as you see fit. If you have trouble with these 32nd note patterns, first do them in a slow 8 beat count time signature then build up to a slow $\frac{4}{4}$. Build up to a tempo of at least 92 BPM. For variety in sight-reading, some variations in notation are included (such as abbreviations).

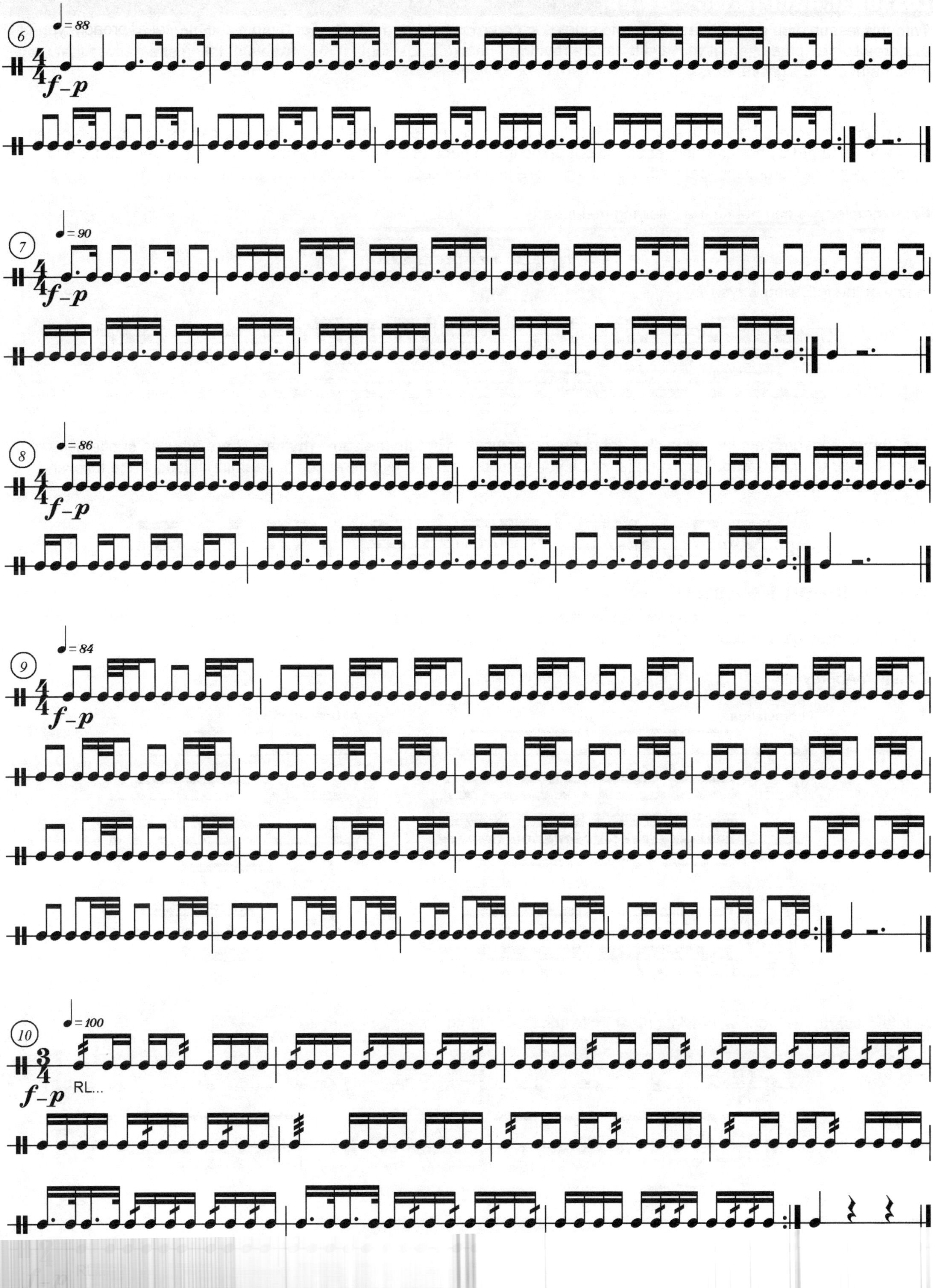
6
♩ = 88
4/4
f–p
7
♩ = 90
4/4
f–p
8
♩ = 86
4/4
f–p
9
♩ = 84
4/4
f–p
10
♩ = 100
3/4
f–p
RL...

Lesson 6: Alternative Notation

Throughout this series, I have used common notation variations where appropriate. This challenging lesson reviews and explores some of the alternative ways to notate rhythm. The exercises contain reasonable notation alternatives that may trick the average sight-reader.

Duration

As a drummer, you strike your instrument which has a pre-determined duration. Although you can use a staccato or legato stroke to try to get a shorter or longer sound out of the instrument, in general, you use a regular stroke no matter what duration note the composer specified. Therefore, there are often several ways to notate the same rhythm.

For example, you can notate the following measure:

In any of the following ways:

The above measures are just examples; there are other ways to notate the same rhythm. There are also subtle differences you will need to understand. For example, see if you can spot the subtle differences in beaming I used in the following three measures:

Abbreviation Review

One bar over a note is an abbreviation that indicates to play eighth notes for the duration of the note. Two bars indicate 16th notes; three bars indicate 32nd notes, etc.

Common Abbreviations:

A dotted quarter with one abbreviation bar indicates three eighth notes, for example:

Common Alternative Notation Review

Study each motif below so that you will better understand the various ways composers can write rhythm. You play all the rhythms in a row from left to right the same for snare and all percussion where the duration is predetermined.

Alternative Notation Exercises

The following exercises are tricky, and although it is doubtful you will ever run into a real percussion part that is as tricky to read, you will occasionally run into small sections that use the notation contained within these exercises.

Traditional Ties

These traditional tie exercises are a follow up to the lesson in volume two titled, "The Traditional Tie".

Odd Beaming and Phrase Markings

Sometimes you will encounter non-standard beaming (odd grouping of notes). You can safely assume there is a purpose for such notation and interpret it appropriately. For example, you can interpret odd beaming as phrasing and play the drum part accordingly by moving the natural stress points of the measure to the beginning of the beamed group of notes.

Exercise #4 notates exercise #3 using more traditional dotted phrase markings along with staccato marks to notate the same piece of music, but two BPM slower – learn to feel the difference between 120 BPM and 118 BPM. Because of the difficulty in reading odd beam groups, composers sometimes use phrase markings rather than odd beaming. Although phrase markings are more common with pitched instruments, on occasion, you will encounter them in drum parts.

Abbreviations

The following exercise uses eighth note and sixteenth note abbreviation notation. Measure 1 uses the added staccato notation used by some composers, which clearly shows the number of strokes for the value indicated.

This lesson includes both alternative time signature notation and an exploration of some of the more exotic time signatures. Because time signatures dictate the fundamental rhythmic composition of music, composers often explore alternative and unusual time signatures. This lesson categorizes the types of time signatures and explores some of the alternative time signatures you might come across. In general, the exercises in this lesson will use simple rhythms that follow the implied stresses of the time signature along with accents, flams, and closed rolls to explore the feel implied by the time signature. The exercises in this lesson stress that notated notes represent durations and rhythm is simply a mathematical relationship of note durations played at a given tempo.

Meters and Time Signatures

You can use the terms meter, time, and time signature interchangeably. They speak to the rhythmic breakdown of each measure and indicate an implied stress pattern within each measure.

Perfect Time (2, 3, 4, 6, 8...)

Perfect time refers to time signatures where the beat group is divisible by 2 or 3. In other words, the top number is a 2, 3, 4, 6, 8, 9, 10, 12, etc. Perfect time can be either simple or compound.

Simple Perfect Time ($\frac{2}{4}$, $\frac{3}{4}$, $\frac{4}{4}$...)

Simple perfect time refers to time signatures where the beat count is naturally divisible by two. Examples of simple perfect time include $\frac{2}{4}$, $\frac{3}{4}$, $\frac{4}{4}$, $\frac{2}{1}$, $\frac{3}{1}$, $\frac{3}{2}$, $\frac{3}{8}$, etc. Simple perfect time also refers to $\frac{6}{8}$ when taken in six (the eighth note is the beat count).

Compound Perfect Time ($\frac{6}{8}$, $\frac{9}{8}$, $\frac{12}{8}$...)

Compound perfect time refers to time signatures where the beat count is naturally divisible by three. Examples of compound perfect time include $\frac{6}{8}$, $\frac{9}{8}$, $\frac{12}{8}$, etc. where the beat count is a dotted quarter note (three eighth notes) and others such as $\frac{6}{4}$, $\frac{9}{4}$, $\frac{12}{4}$, $\frac{18}{8}$, etc. where the beat count is a dotted half note (three quarter notes).

Imperfect Time (5, 7, 11...)

Imperfect time refers to time signatures where the beat group is not divisible by 2 or 3. In other words, the top number is a 5, 7, 11, 13, 17, 19, 23, 25, etc. Examples of a few imperfect time signatures include $\frac{5}{4}$, $\frac{7}{8}$, $\frac{13}{16}$, and 23/32.

Note in Beat Duration

Since the bottom number of a time signature indicates which note gets the beat duration, some composers are starting to use the actual note. Using an actual note in the bottom number clearly indicates whether you should take a time signature like 6/8 six, simple time, where the eighth note gets the beat count, or in two, compound time, where the dotted quarter note gets the beat count.

The following are some examples of using a note in the bottom of a time signature:

Simple Perfect Time Exercises

Compound Perfect Time Exercises

These exercises use a note as the bottom number of the meter to indicate to take the dotted quarter as the beat count.

Imperfect Time Exercises

In general, imperfect time is split into groups of 2 and 3 notes. For example, you can split $\frac{5}{8}$ into either 2+3 or 3+2 eighth notes. You can split $\frac{7}{8}$ into 3+2+2, 2+2+3, or 2+3+2 eighth notes. See if you can feel the split taken on these exercises.

Half Note Time Signatures

In half note beat time signatures, the beat duration is the half note so the half note gets the beat count. When you play $\frac{4}{4}$ in cut time (alla breve time), you change the time signature from $\frac{4}{4}$ to $\frac{2}{2}$.

Whole Note Time Signatures

In whole note beat time signatures, the beat duration is the whole note. In exercise #13, the first and last note is a double whole note. A double whole can be represented by 𝇎 or 𝅜 and is equal to eight quarter notes. In measure 3 of exercise #14 is a double whole rest on beats 2 and 3. A double whole rest is represented by 𝄺.

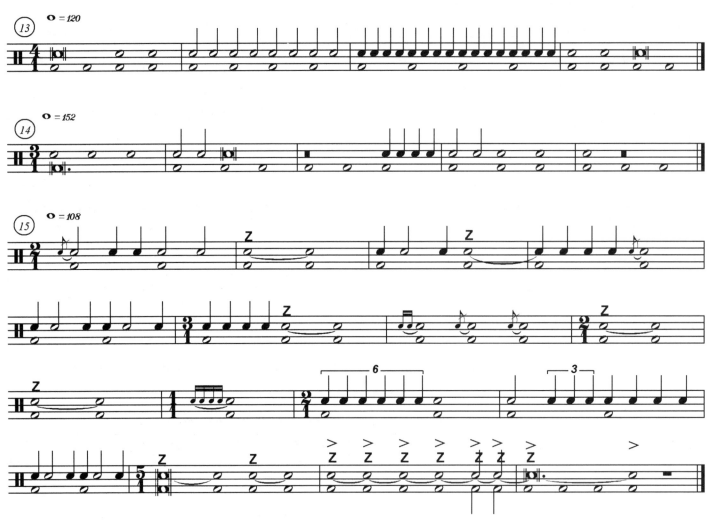

32nd Note Time Signatures

In 32nd note beat time signatures, the beat duration is the 32nd note. In exercise #16, I used extended beams and half stems along with rests to more clearly represent the rhythms. Exercise #17 is an example of the type of passage you are likely to see if you do come across a 32nd note time signatures.

64th Note Time Signatures

In 64th note beat time signatures, the beat duration is the 64th note. In exercise #18, the tempo is 60 BPM for a 16th note (120 BPM for 32nd notes and 240 BPM for 64th notes). Exercise #19 explores quintuplet rhythms.

No Beat Duration Specified

Some composers are adopting the practice of not specifying the beat duration. With this practice, they specify the beat group only and require you to analyze the measure to determine the beat count.

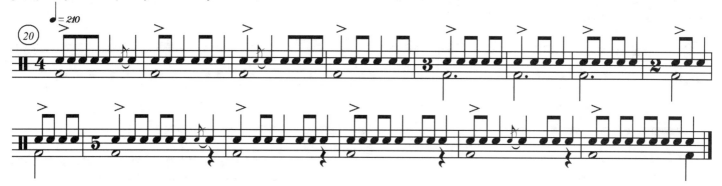

Composite Time Signatures

A composite time signature brings together two or more time signatures into a single measure. In all cases, the composer could have specified a single time signature but will opt for a composite time signature to indicate the beat group within a measure. In example #21, the $\frac{3}{8}$ + $\frac{4}{8}$ composite time signature is really just $\frac{7}{8}$ grouped as 3+4.

Dotted Barlines

A *dotted barline* or *dashed barline* divides a measure into metrical groups. Composers use dotted barlines within a metrically complex measure to provide metrical guidelines. These guidelines aid your interpretation of the music. Although beams and phrase markings sometimes have an impact on a measure's stress points, dotted barlines usually do not. Dotted barlines are particularly helpful in very syncopated imperfect time signatures such as 5/8, 7/2, and 17/16.

Lesson 8: 64th Notes in 16th Note Time Signatures

The purpose of this lesson is to get you comfortable reading 16th note time signatures. You will rarely see a complete piece written in a 16th note time signature. More commonly, you will see a section of a piece in a 16th note time signature.

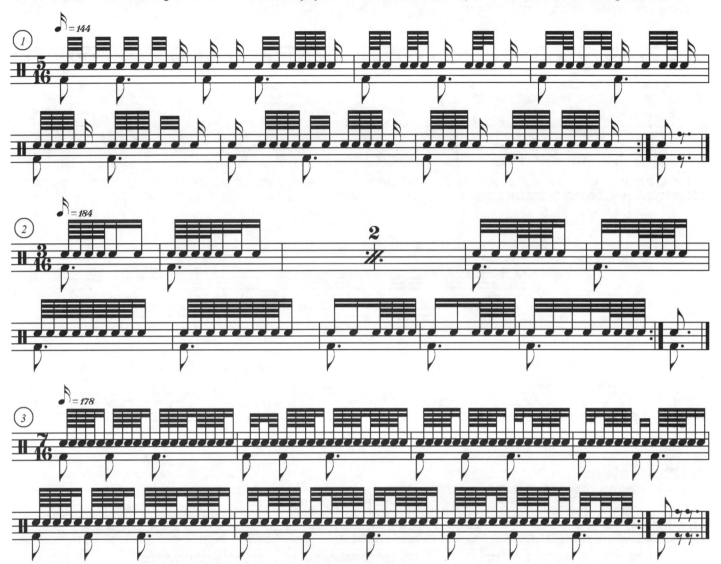

Counting rhythm is important, but you must be able to both count and feel rhythm. Often, rhythm is played too fast to count. The following exercise is another one you should both count and feel. Learn to feel the 2, 3, 4, 5, 6, and 7 beat rhythms in this exercise.

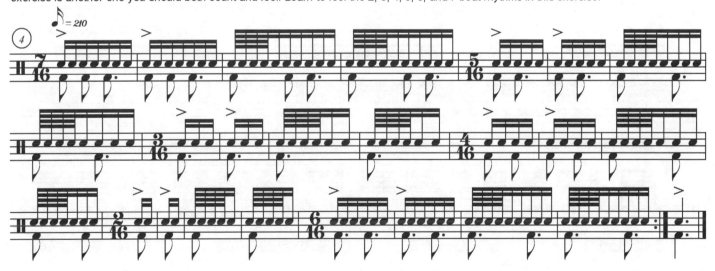

The purpose of this lesson is to get you comfortable reading 32nd note time signatures. Although you may never see a complete piece written in a 32nd note time signature, the experience you gain from this lesson will help you with your fundamental understanding of rhythm theory.

This lesson reviews the rhythms covered to this point but this time in odd times.

The next six lessons explore dividing notes and through practice you will gain the ability to play any rhythm at various tempos well. In lessons 13, 14, and 15, you focus on dividing a single note at various tempos. Lessons 16, 17, and 18 explore dividing 2 or more notes.

About Prime Numbers and Drums

A prime number is an integer greater than one and only divisible by one and itself. The first prime numbers are 2, 3, 5, 7, and 11. Memorize the feel of dividing any duration into the first five prime numbers. All other subdivisions of a note are simply multiples of a prime number.

Prime Number Exercises

As a musician, you have to develop the ability to divide a note into whatever division is called for. With common time rhythm, you simply divide by two. A whole note divides into two half notes. Half notes divide into two quarter-notes. Quarter notes divide into two eighth-notes, etc. When you first learned triplets, they "felt" funny because they divide by three instead of by two. After you learned triplets, you found sixes, which is two 16th note triplets, relatively easy to learn.

The exercises in this lesson only use quarter notes and prime numbered tuples. They are among the most difficult exercises in this method book. The easiest way to master these exercises is to download the audio files from play-drums.com. Exercise #1 uses the clearer ratio notation while the other two use the traditional notation. You can read the ratio notation in exercise #1 as play three in the place of two 8th notes, play five in the place of four 16th notes, play seven in the place four 16th notes, and play eleven in the place of eight 32nd notes.

Lesson 12: Rhythmic Mnemonics

A mnemonic is a word or phrase used to assist memory. For example, musicians often learn to use "Good Boys Do Fine Always" for the lines on the bass clef. A rhythmic mnemonic is a word or phrase used to help you remember the "feel" of a rhythm. For example, drum instructors often use "ma-ma da-da" to help young students learn double strokes (R-R L-L) to help convey the smooth even playing of the notes. Although you need to learn to play without counting and without the aid of mnemonics, using mnemonics while learning a piece can be helpful. Practice these exercises at slow tempos.

# of Notes	Tuple	Suggested Mnemonic	Notes
2	Duplet	pizza	
3	Triplet	strawberry	
4	Quadruplet	double pizza	Some use "pizza pizza" since a quadruplet is really just two duplets.
5	Quintuplet	hippopotamus	
6	Sextuplet	strawberry-strawberry	Some use "hippopotamuses" but a sextuplet is really just two triplets.
7	Septuplet	Boysenberry Turnover	
8	Octuplet	N/A	You can use supercalifragilistic but nothing is suggested since an octuplet is really just four duplets or two quadruplets and typically you play 8 notes too fast to say a mnemonic.

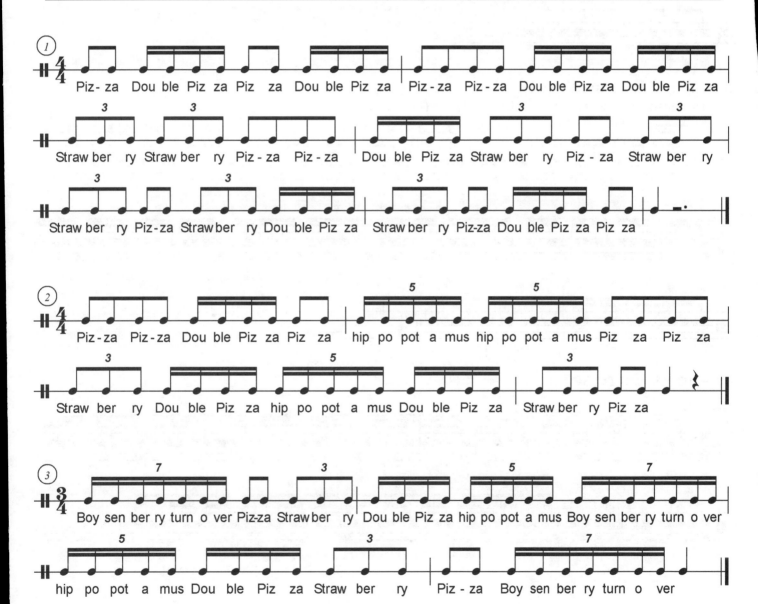

This lesson covers dividing quarter notes from 2 to 14 at various tempos. Because it is important that you have the ability to both feel and count rhythm, practice these exercises both counting the quarter note and not counting. Also, you should practice playing these exercises both tapping your foot and not tapping your foot.

2 to 6 to 2 Exercise

Sixes along with quintuplets and triplets will likely become the core of your advanced rhythm playing. You can think of sixes as one triplet per eighth note or two sixteenths per eighth note in an eighth note triplet. Since 5 is a prime number, you just have to memorize the feel of a quintuplet.

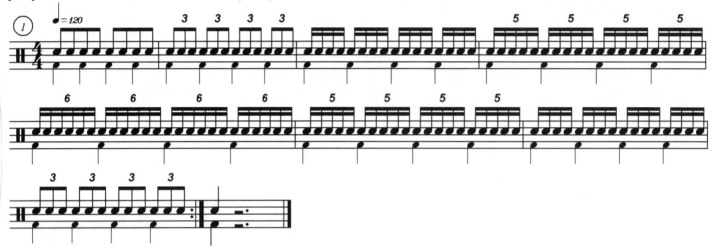

3 to 7 to 3 Exercise

At slow to medium tempos, you can utilize septuplets (7s) with a little effort.

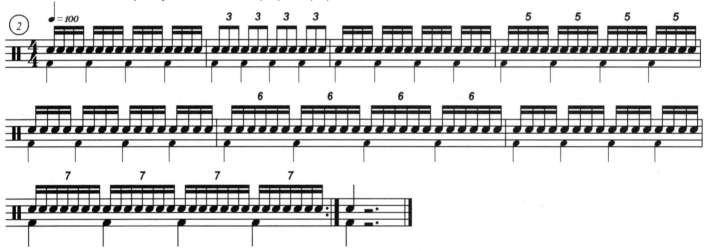

8s and 9s Exercise

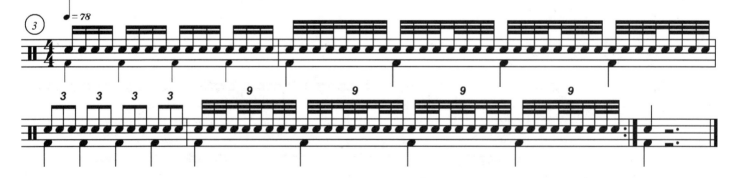

10s and 12s Exercise

You can leverage your knowledge of a quintuplet (5 notes) with a 10-tuple because a 10-tuple is a quintuplet (5 notes) per eighth note. In addition, you can leverage your knowledge of a triplet with a 12-tuple because a 12-tuple is a triplet per 16th note.

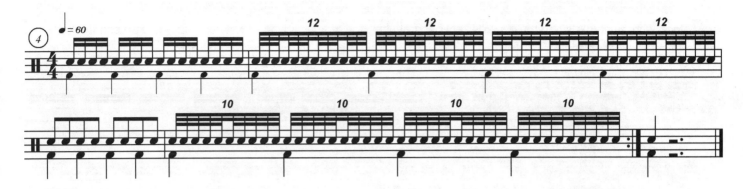

1 to 12 Breakdown Exercise

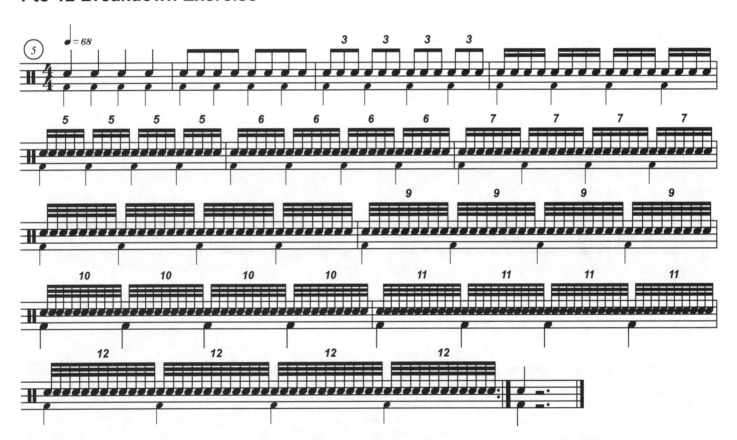

12 to 1 Breakdown Exercise
Exercise #6 uses the clearer ratio notation.

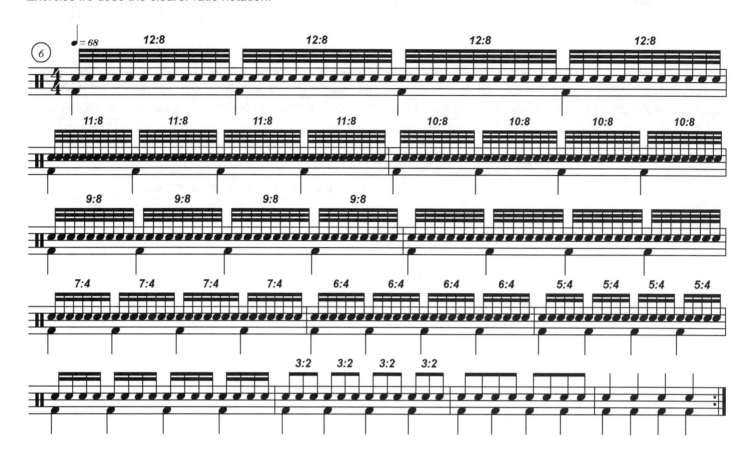

10, 12, 14 Doubles Exercise
This next exercise uses double strokes along with quintuplets, sextuplets, and septuplets to perform 10, 12, and 14 note tuples.

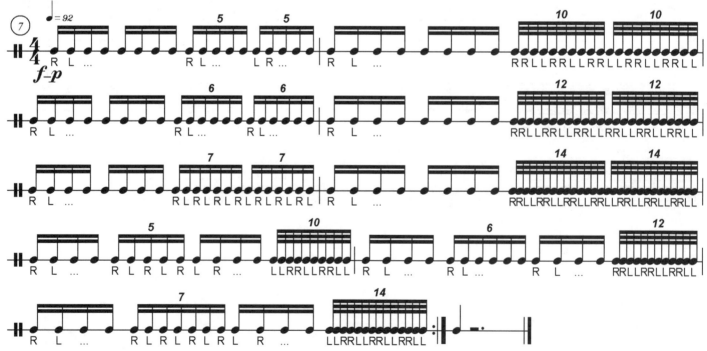

Lesson 14: Advanced ¼ Note Triplet Exercises

This lesson covers dividing two quarter notes into a quarter note triplet and builds on the lesson titled "1/4 Note Triplets" in volume two.

Lesson 15: Advanced Tuples

Tuples are not just limited to replacing one beat count with a duplet, triplet, etc. With a tuple, you can take any note or set of notes and replace it with a tuple of any given number of notes. You replace a section of the current meter's beat count with a superimposed meter. This lesson explores replacing 2, 3, 4, and 5 quarter notes as well as 2 and 3 dotted quarter notes with a tuple.

Leverage Your Knowledge

When playing complex odd tuples, sometimes you can leverage the notes surrounding the most complex sections to help you more accurately perform the section. For example, in the lesson titled "Easy Breakdowns", you learned to play a septuplet (7 notes) a little faster than a sextuplet (6 notes).

Transition Measures

The easiest way to master the timing of these exercises is to download the audio files from play-drums.com. However, all of the exercises in this lesson use an accented pattern to lead into the complex tuple. With the accented pattern, you can easily master the timing required to play the complex tuples. In addition, if you write your own drum parts, this is an excellent technique for transitioning into a complex tuple. Learn to feel the upcoming tuple pattern within the accent pattern that precedes the tuple.

Superimposed Time Signatures

If you have trouble interpreting the notation of tuples, irregular note divisions, try to understand the implied superimposed time signature and the relation of the beat count. For example, take the following snippet:

When rewritten in its superimposed meter below, is perhaps easier to understand:

Replace Beat Count

Another technique for correctly interpreting tuples is to replace the beat count with an easier to play beat count (at least in your head). For example, in exercise #5 if you tap your foot on count 1 of each measure you will find the exercise easier to play. This technique works with all the exercises in this lesson.

Alternative Notation

The exercises in this lesson utilize the most common notation for tuples. However, since composers are human and the rules of tuple notation are flexible, you will come across variations. For example, you play the following four measures the same. They contain common notation variations for the first set of exercises -- 8th Note Quintuplets (5:4). Make note of the use of ratio notation in measures 1 and 3. For measure 1 you read the ratio notation as play five notes in the place of four 8th notes.

As a second example, the following measures all represent playing 7 notes in the space of two quarters and although measures 3 and 4 are more correctly notated, some composers will use the other variations. Read the first two measures as play seven notes in the space of two quarter-notes. Read measures 3 and 4 as play seven notes in the space of four 8th notes. Read the final two measures as play seven notes in the space of eight 16th notes.

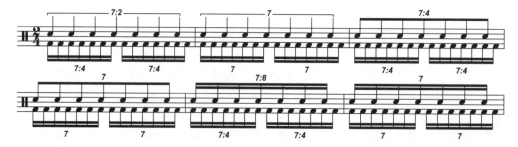

The next lesson, titled "Tuple Problem Areas" explores more problem areas with reading and performing tuples.

Replace Two Quarter Notes

This first set of exercises explores the replacing of two quarter-notes with a single quintuplet (5) or septuplet (7).

8th Note Quintuplet (5:4)

Play five notes in the place of four 8th notes.

You play an 8th note quintuplet slightly slower than triplets.

Exercise #1 is an accent preparation exercise in which the accent pattern matches an 8th note quintuplet (5:4).

8th Note Septuplet (7:4)

Play seven notes in the place of four 8th notes.

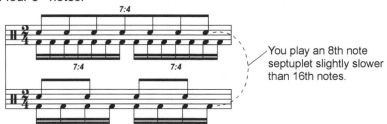

You play an 8th note septuplet slightly slower than 16th notes.

Exercise #6 is an accent preparation exercise in which the accent pattern matches an 8th note septuplet (7:4).

Replace Three Quarter Notes

This next section explores the replacing of three quarter notes with various tuples.

Eighth Note Quintuplet (5:6)

Play five notes in the place of three quarter notes (six 8th notes).

You play an 8th note quintuplet (5:6) slightly slower than eighth notes.

Eighth Note Septuplet (7:6)

Play seven notes in the place of eight 8th notes.

You play an 8th note septuplet (7:6) slightly faster than 8th notes.

Replace Four Quarter Notes

This next section explores the replacing of four quarter-notes with various tuples.

Half Note Triplet (3:2)

Play three notes in the place of two half notes.

Quarter Note Quintuplet (5:4)

Play five notes in the place of four quarter-notes.

Eighth Note Septuplet (7:8)

Play seven notes in the place of eight 8th notes (four quarter notes).

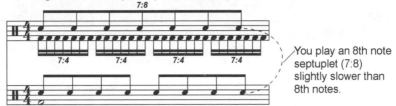

You play an 8th note septuplet (7:8) slightly slower than 8th notes.

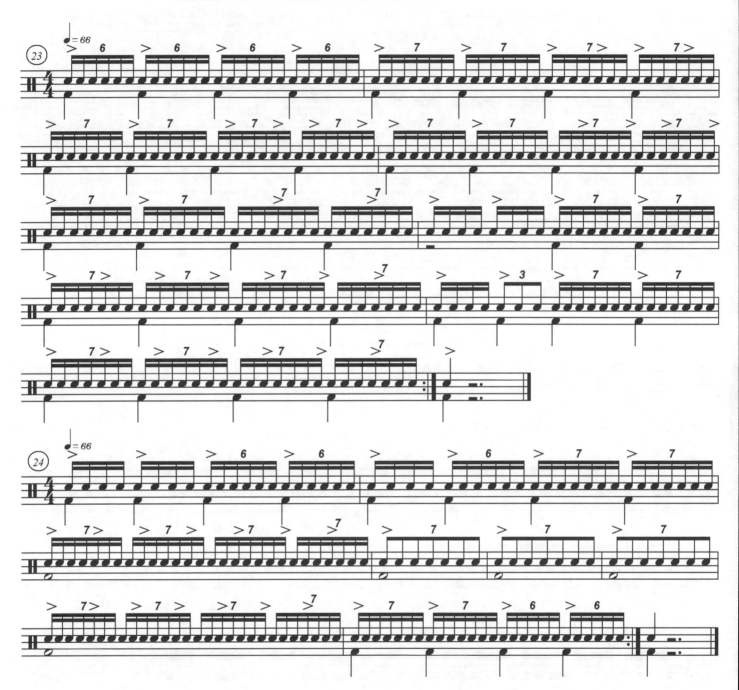

Replace Five Quarter Notes

This next section explores the replacing of four quarter-notes with various tuples.

Quarter Note Triplet (3:5)
Play three notes in the place of five quarter-notes.

Quarter Note Quadruplet (4:5)
Play four notes in the place of five quarter-notes.

Quarter Note Triplet (3:5) Exercises

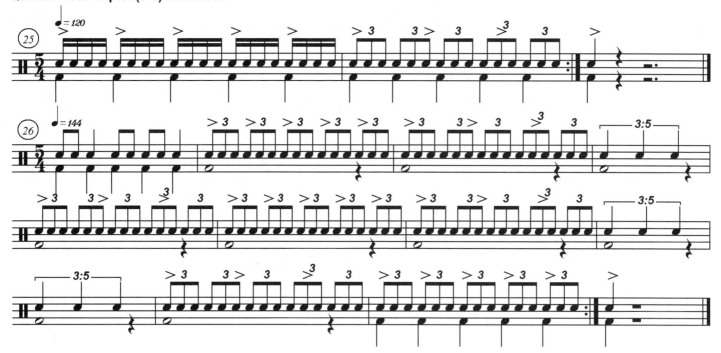

Quarter Note Quadruplet (4:5) Exercises

Quarter Note Sextuplet (6:5)

Play six notes in the place of five quarter-notes.

Quarter Note Septuplet (7:5)

Play four notes in the place of five quarter-notes.

Quarter Note Sextuplet (6:5) Exercises

Quarter Note Septuplet (7:5) Exercises

Replace Two Dotted Quarter Notes

This next section explores the replacing of two dotted quarter notes with various tuples.

Quarter Note Quintuplet (5:6)

Play five notes in the place of two dotted quarter notes (six 8th notes).

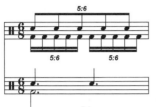

Eighth Note Septuplet (7:6)

Play seven notes in the place of two dotted quarter notes (six 8th notes).

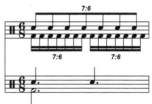

Quarter Note Quintuplet (5:6) Exercises

Eighth Note Septuplet (7:6) Exercises

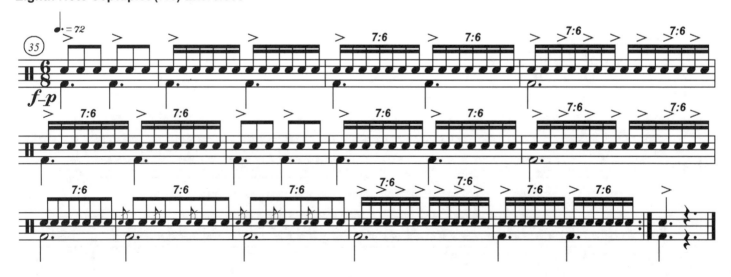

Replace Three Dotted Quarter Notes

This next section explores the replacing of three dotted quarter notes with various tuples.

Quarter Note Quadruplet (8:9)
Play eight notes in the place of three dotted quarter notes (nine 8th notes).

Eighth Note Quintuplet (5:9)
Play five notes in the place of three dotted quarter notes (nine 8th notes).

Eighth Note Septuplet (7:9)
Play seven notes in the place of three dotted quarter notes (nine 8th notes).

Quarter Note Quadruplet (8:9) Exercises
Play eight notes in the form of quarters and eighths in the place of three dotted quarter notes (nine 8th notes).

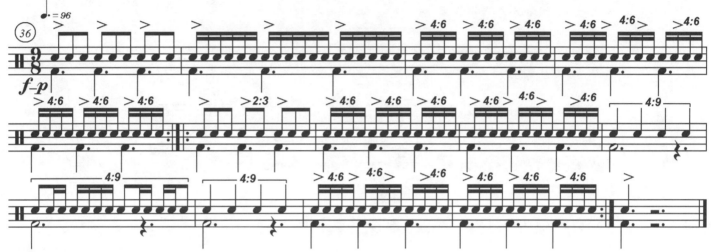

Eighth Note Quintuplet (5:9) Exercises

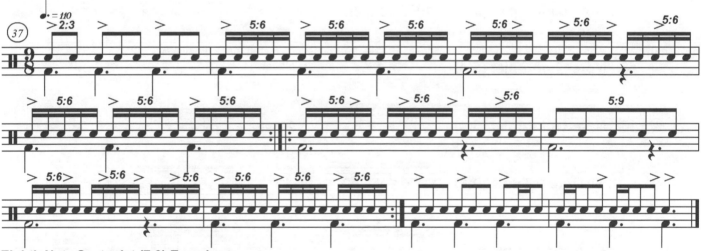

Eighth Note Septuplet (7:9) Exercises

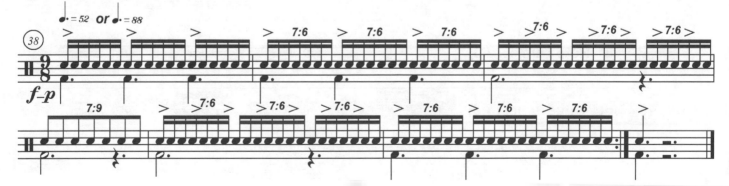

The rules guiding the usage of tuples are very flexible -- perhaps too flexible. When notating a tuple you can take any duration in the given time signature and divide it by any numbered tuple. Theoretically, you can replace three quarter notes with seven 16th notes. Because of this freedom, reading tuples is often confusing and unclear. This lesson provides guidance in interpreting commonly and uncommonly notated tuples. I borrowed many of the examples in this lesson from published music but changed the music enough to protect the guilty.

Common Beaming of Tuples

The most common way to beam tuples in common time is to beam a tuple with the beaming scheme of the next lower common time beam. For example, since 8th note triplets replace two 8th notes, you use a single beam. For compound time such as $\frac{6}{8}$, the most common way to beam a tuple is with the beaming scheme of the next higher common time beam. For example, since an 8th note duplet replaces three 8th notes, you use a single beam.

Common Beaming Examples

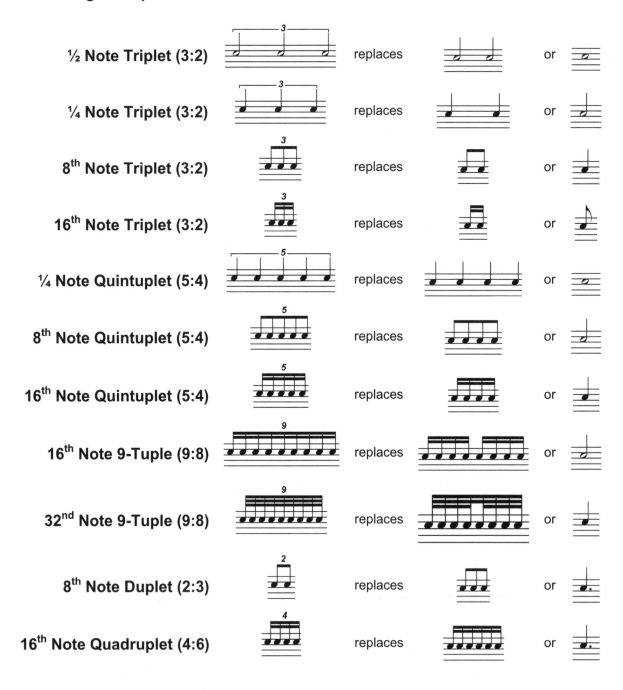

Uncommon Beaming Examples

In the following example #1, the 16th note 9-tuple replaces four 16th notes or one quarter note. You know this because the composer has notated the first three beat counts clearly. However, since there are eight 32nd notes to a quarter note (the next lower beaming scheme from nine), the tuple would be more clear if represented by 32nd notes as in the revised version. As #1 is written, some musicians may believe the time signature is actually 5/4 time.

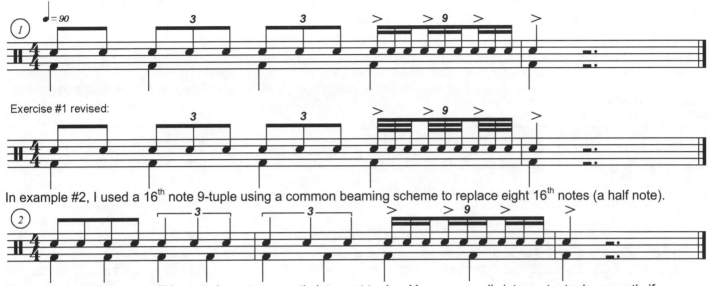

Exercise #1 revised:

In example #2, I used a 16th note 9-tuple using a common beaming scheme to replace eight 16th notes (a half note).

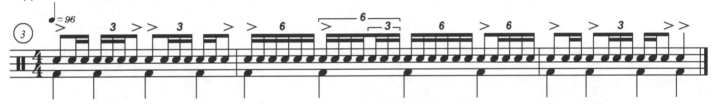

When sight reading, you will have to learn to correctly interpret tuples. You can usually interpret a tuple correctly if you analyze the measure as a whole.

Compound Tuples

Sometimes, composers overuse tuples when a change in time signature is clearer. Take for example, this very complex snippet:

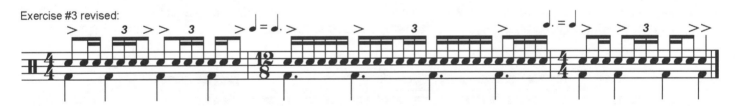

If you have trouble playing a passage like this, in your mind try translating the music into its superimposed time signature. When revised as follows, the above very complex snippet becomes a very easy to read snippet. To be clear, both are technically correct and you play both identically. Notice I kept the beat count consistent with the quarter note equals a dotted quarter note notation.

Exercise #3 revised:

Example #4 is a very complex section of music that is much easier to read and understand when written in a more compatible time signature as demonstrated in the two revisions. Therefore, although you may encounter a complex piece of music with layered tuples, if you learn to convert them in your mind to a more compatible time signature, you may have an easier time interpreting and performing them. (The bass drum part is included for reference only.)

Exercise #4 revision 1:

Exercise #4 revision 2:

Tuples Crossing Measures

In exercise #5, the notation is correct but clearer and less complex than in the revised version.

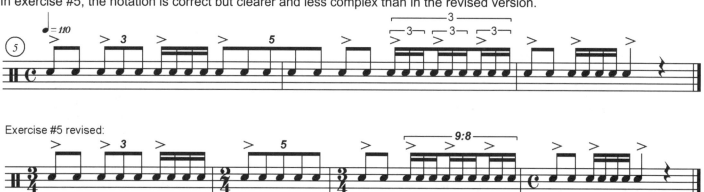

Exercise #5 revised:

Tuples that start on the Upbeat

When tuples start on upbeats and other odd stress points, you can aid your interpretation by marking the start and finish of the tuple duration before you to play the tuple. The following exercise stresses this point.

Lesson 17: Shifting Beat Groups

This lesson builds on the lesson titled "Switching Beat Groups" in volume two. Sometimes composers use several time signatures to establish a moving shifting pattern. This exercise uses the legato stroke (a very slight accent) to stress the beat group of the given time signature. Play exercise #1 on the rim (you may need to count out loud a few times), play exercises #2 and #3 on the drum, counting to yourself, then practice without counting at all (feel the music).

Lesson 18: Switching Beat Duration (Same Beat Count)

To play music that changes beat duration, you must understand the beat count relationship of the two time signatures. In the following exercises you keep the same beat count tempo but switch between simple and compound time (♩ = ♩.). For example, in 4/4 the quarter note gets the beat count and in 12/8 the dotted quarter note gets the beat count.

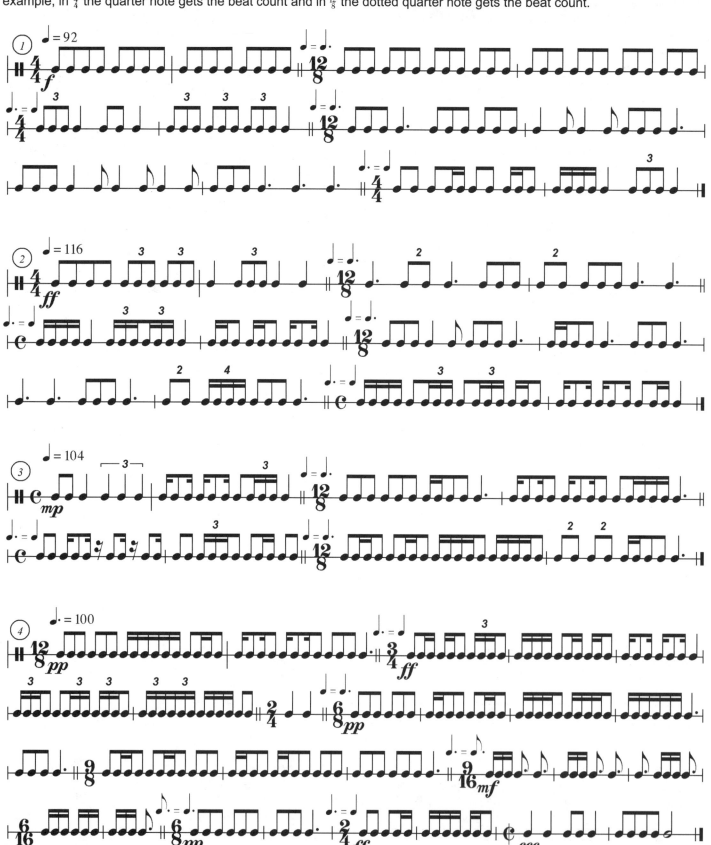

Lesson 19: Switching Beat Duration

Through progressively more difficult exercises, you will learn how to switch beat duration. Switching beat duration with an ♪ = ♪ beat count allows the composer the freedom to create complex time signature movement within a piece. Since the time signature influences rhythm, this is a powerful tool for creating music with a non-common time feel. In addition, the composer can extend or cut short common time measures in order to achieve a temporary non-common time feel. In the following examples, the tempo of the beat count changes depending on the current beat duration. Eighth notes (1-&-2-&) in $\frac{2}{4}$ are played at the same speed as eighth notes (1-2-3-4-5-6) in $\frac{6}{8}$. With these exercises, a note gets the same duration no matter what the time signature.

47

This next exercise stresses switching from $\frac{3}{4}$ and $\frac{2}{4}$ playing 16ths and quintuplets to playing 5/16 time with a sixteenth equaling a sixteenth. To be clear, the quintuplets in the $\frac{3}{4}$ and $\frac{2}{4}$ measures are faster than 16ths in the 5/16 measures and the 16ths in the $\frac{3}{4}$ and $\frac{2}{4}$ measures equal the sixteenths in 5/16 measures.

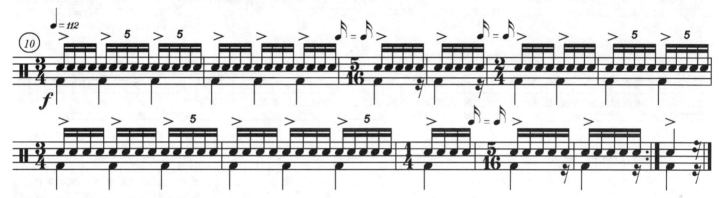

A $\frac{2}{2}$, Cut Time (¢), $\frac{4}{4}$, 8/8 Exercise

Although a composer could easily write the following exercise entirely in $\frac{4}{4}$, it uses alternative equivalent time signatures to point out the desired different stress patterns in each section. This exercise contains three fundamentally different sections. In the $\frac{2}{2}$ (or cut time) section, the desired beat count stress is the half note and has an overall slower feel to it than the other two sections. In the $\frac{4}{4}$ section, the desired beat count stress is the quarter note and has an overall faster feel. In the third section, I based the desired beat count stress on a syncopated eighth note pattern where I was looking to group each measure in 3+3+2.

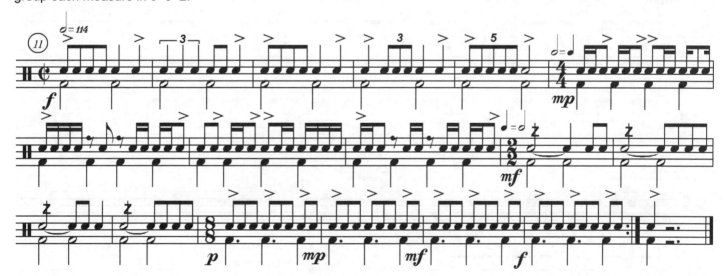

Mixing Same Beat Count and switching beat duration

The following exercise alternates between perfect and imperfect time and between simple and compound time. If not specified, assume an 8th note in one time signature equals an 8th note in another. To be clear, the triplet in measure 16 is the same speed as the 8th notes in measure 14.

Lesson 20: No Time Signature

The purpose of this lesson is to help you let go of counting and to explore feeling rhythm and rhythmic breakdowns. Do not attempt to count this exercise -- just feel the rhythms. Although I hid the various time signatures and measure barlines, they do exist. However, do not add them to this exercise, as the point of the exercise is to explore reading rhythmic breakdowns relative to each other. Your only indication to start this exercise is a tempo mark of 120 BPM. All other notes are relative to the preceding notes. This exercise starts out grouping on two eighth notes (simple time), moves to occasionally losing an eighth note (imperfect time), to grouping in 3 (similar to compound time), then unusual grouping such as 4, 5, 6, 7, and 8 eighth notes. Finally, it ends with grouping of 16th notes with accents and flams.

Lesson 21: Flat Flams and Polyrhythms

A *polyrhythm* is the playing of two separate rhythms played against one another (at the same time). A *polyrhythmic rudiment* is the playing of one rhythm with your right hand while playing a different rhythm in your left hand. You can use polyrhythmic rudiments with two different percussion instruments (one on each hand). For example, play your right hand on a cowbell (or snare rim) and your left hand on the snare drum. For this lesson, I categorized polyrhythmic rudiments as simple, syncopated, and tuple.

Flat Flams

A *flat flam* is a two-handed drum stroke in which both left and right hand strokes play at the same time – similar to a regular flam, but promote the grace note to a full stroke and strike both strokes at the same time.

Legend

Simple Polyrhythms

A *simple polyrhythm* does not use tuples and stays compliant with the meter. The following exercises introduce some common simple polyrhythms.

Syncopated Polyrhythms

A *syncopated polyrhythm* is the playing of two separate rhythms played against one another with at least one of the rhythms not compliant with the meter. Usually, one hand plays a meter compliant rhythm while the other does not. However, there are no rules guiding this, you have a lifetime to explore syncopated polyrhythms.

Bossa Nova

The following exercise explores syncopated polyrhythms using a bossa nova beat.

Tuple Polyrhythms

A *tuple polyrhythm* is the playing of two separate rhythms each from a contrasting meter played against one another. For composers, the trick is to find a way to use them musically. Tuple polyrhythms tend to sound like noise and are effective when composers use them in that manor. In addition, many composers find interesting and musical ways to apply them.

Common Tuple Polyrhythms (3:2, 3:4, 3:5, 4:5)

The following exercises get you started playing tuple polyrhythms. Exercise 8 stresses the most common tuple polyrhythm of 3 against 2. For exercise 8, tap your foot on the quarter note beat. For the rest of the exercises, tap your foot at the beginning of the measure. Experiment with tuple polyrhythms in various meters and at various tempos.

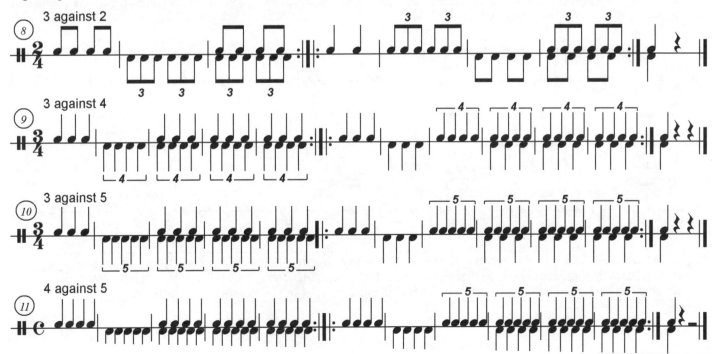

Appendix A: Warm-Up Set 3

Use these exercises as a warm up to your daily practice sessions. Play each warm up exercise at a fast as comfortable tempo using relaxed muscles. If you feel the slightest tightness or pain, stop and start over at a slightly slower tempo. In order to warm up your mind as well as your hands, repeat each exercise as indicated. Forcing your mind to track the repeats of each exercise increases your ability to focus. For a more thorough warm up, repeat entire page as needed.

Legato Strokes

This version of the legato exercise builds your confidence with groups of notes from 3 to 12. In addition, it exercises dynamic control and switching beat duration with an 8th equaling an 8th -- play all the 8th notes at the same speed.

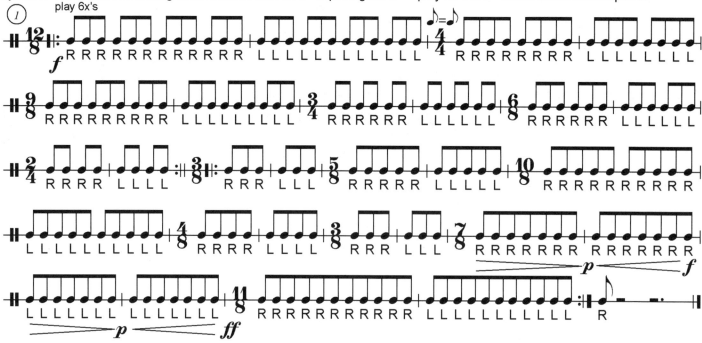

One Handed Accents

This exercises works on your accent attack stroke and follow up stroke. Take this exercise at a comfortable and somewhat slow tempo.

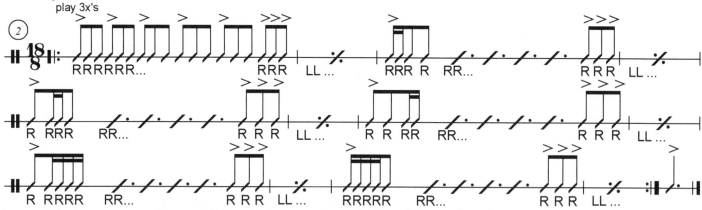

> ***Notation Notes*** The above exercise makes use of stems-up rhythmic notation (line heads), dotted single beat repeats, and measure repeats that switch to your left hand. Also, note the final measure is incomplete, which is non-standard notation -- some composers occasionally leave the last bar incomplete.

Diddles

Mixed Alternating Singles

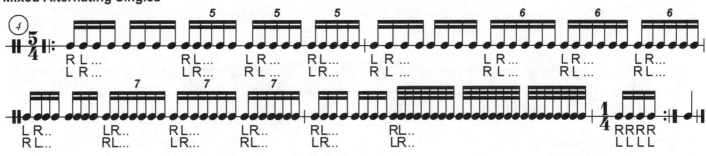

Accent Study

This next exercise stresses timing the various strokes: accents, flams, closed roll, and double strokes. The first time through, play the accents as written. Then replace **accents** with **flams, closed roll** strokes, and then **double strokes**.

Odd Sticking

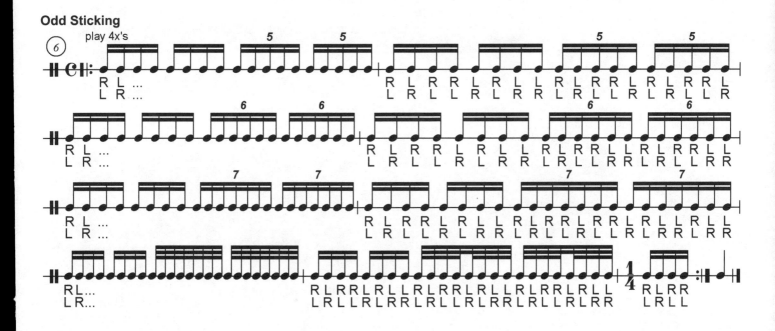

Closed and Open Roll Warm Up

Mixed Rolls

Start each practice session with a thorough warm-up (see Appendix A) followed by some chop building using this material. How long you spend on this appendix and how many variations you exercise depends on how much time you have and how much control and dexterity you wish to develop.

Sharpen the Saw

In addition to performing these exercises as written, you can use these rhythmic accent patterns for a variety of drumming exercises. The following is a guide you can use with these exercises to sharpen your saw.

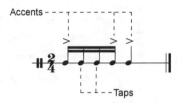

Orchestral Snare:

Using a set of orchestral sticks, try any of the following variations:

1. Play the accents as forte (8" to 12" strokes) and the taps at mezzo forte (6" to 9" strokes).
2. Play the accents as forte and the taps as piano.
3. Lead with your left hand (weak hand).
4. Substitute flams for the accents.
5. Play the accents on right hand and the taps on left hand – play both at same dynamic, no accents.
6. Play the accents on left hand and the taps on right hand – play both at same dynamic, no accents.
7. Instead of taps with accents, play a crush roll with accented crush strokes.
8. Play a crush stroke in place of accents.
9. Play a crush roll in place of taps – keep accents.
10. Choose a few exercises and substitute legato rim shots for the accents.
11. Choose a few exercises and substitute staccato rim shots for the accents.
12. Using a slower tempo, choose a few exercises and substitute a tuple (group of notes) in place of the accent (i.e. a duplet, triplet, quadruplet, quintuplet, etc.)

Rudimental study:

Using a set of heavier sticks, try any of the following variations:

13. Play the accents as forte (8" to 12" strokes) and the taps at mezzo forte (6" to 9" strokes).
14. Play the accents as forte and the taps as piano.
15. Substitute flams for the accents.
16. Substitute diddles (a double stroke) for the accents.
17. Play taps for the accents and diddles for the taps.
18. Instead of taps with accents, play an open roll with accented double strokes.
19. Using a slower tempo, substitute a rudiment in place of the accent. For example, substitute ruffs, triple strokes, Swiss triplets, paradiddles, etc. in place of the accent.
20. Choose a few exercises and substitute legato rim shots for the accents.
21. Choose a few exercises and substitute staccato rim shots for the accents.

Drum Set:

Using a set of drum set sticks, play any of the following variations:

22. Back up accent with the bass drum.
23. Play taps on snare and accents on a tom.
24. Play taps on a tom and accents on snare.
25. Play right-handed accents on low tom and left-handed accents on hi tom.
26. Play accents on hi-hat (staccato splash) with a bass back up.

You can work your hi-hat in with any of the following variations:

27. Choose a variation from 1-25 and keep time with your hi-hat on the beat count.
28. Choose a variation from 1-25 and keep time with your hi-hat on counts 2 and 4.
29. Choose a variation from 1-25 and keep time with your hi-hat on counts 1 and 3.
30. Choose a variation from 1-25 and splash your hi-hat on count 1 (the down beat).

Tempo

In addition to playing theses exercises at a fast as comfortable tempo, work on your precise timing and play them at a slow and comfortable tempo.

> **Reminder** Using relaxed muscles, practice these exercises with a metronome and without a metronome as well as with the audio check patterns available from play-drums.com.

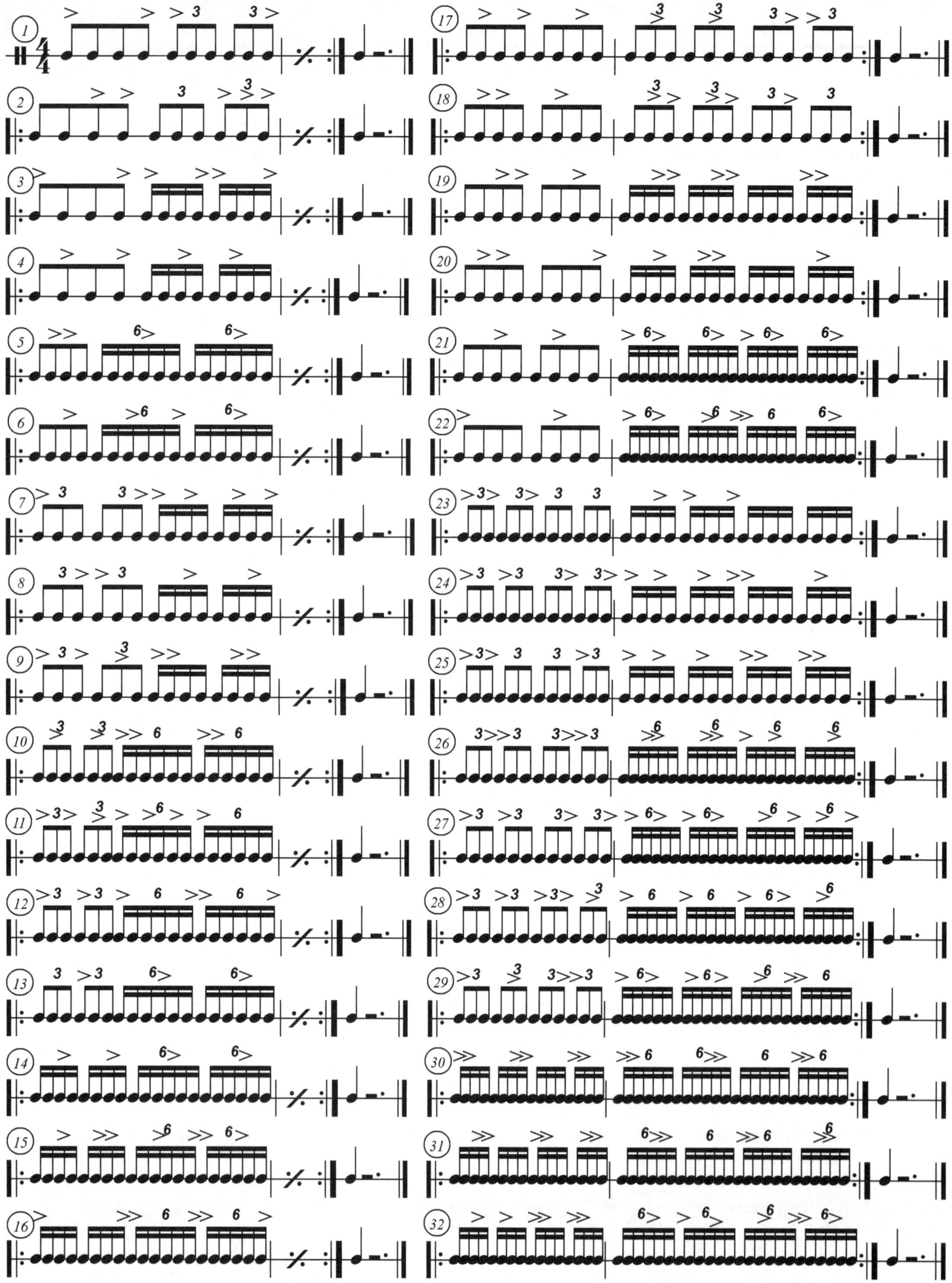

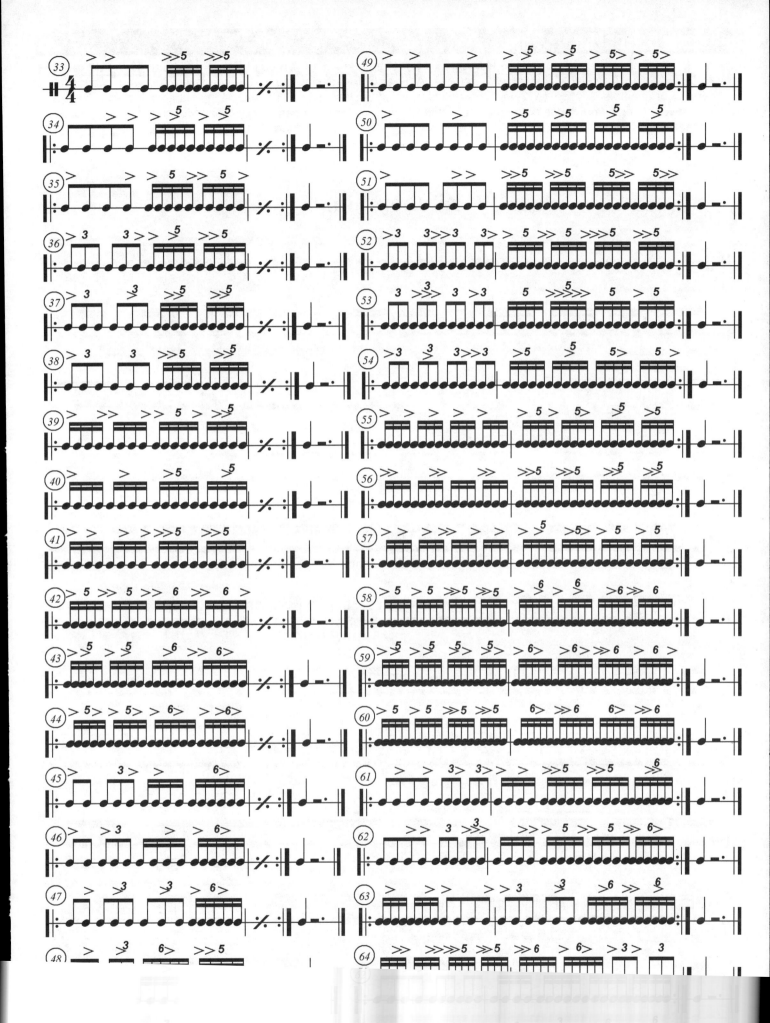

I wrote *Kitchen Sink* to contain most of the elements from this method series. A measure number and an identifier mark the start of each section. The identifier starts with the letter A, B, or C, for volume 1, 2, or 3 respectively, followed by a lesson number(s). For example, section "(A12-14)" contains elements from lessons 12, 13, and 14 in volume 1. You can use this solo to test your overall knowledge of the material covered by this series. If a particular passage is tough for you, you can refer to the lessons for practice exercises. Teachers can use this solo as a placement test for students.

Make sure you review the introductory material to the *Snare Solos* in appendix C in Volume 1. It covers performing a solo, practicing solos, and interpretation.

Kitchen Sink

61